Human Resources

B. Vincent

Published by RWG Publishing, 2021.

While every precaution has been taken in the preparation of this book, the publisher assumes no responsibility for errors or omissions, or for damages resulting from the use of the information contained herein.

HUMAN RESOURCES

First edition. July 9, 2021.

Written by B. Vincent.

Also by B. Vincent

Affiliate Marketing
Affiliate Marketing
Affiliate Marketing

Standalone
Affiliate Recruiting
Business Layoffs & Firings
Business and Entrepreneur Guide
Business Remote Workforce
Career Transition
Project Management
Precision Targeting
Professional Development
Strategic Planning
Content Marketing
Imminent List Building
Getting Past GateKeepers
Banner Ads
Bookkeeping

Bridge Pages
Business Acquisition
Business Bogging
Marketing Automation
Better Meetings
Conversion Optimization
Creative Solutions
Employee Recruitment
Startup Capital
Employee Mentoring
Servant Leadership
Human Resources
Team Building

Human Resources

Lawrence Bossidy once said, Nothing we do is a higher priority than recruiting and creating individuals. Toward the day's end, you bet on individuals not on methodologies. Furthermore, Steve Wynn discloses to us human asset isn't what we do. It's what maintains our business. Individuals are undoubtedly the main asset in any business. The accomplishment of your association depends on the people who come in consistently and put in the work. So it makes sense that your HR division is apparently the main offices in your organization. Consider the big picture. Your HR directors and group are trusted with the consideration of the association's most valuable resource from the beginning to end from the underlying enrolling, confirming and recruiting, to the onboarding, to preparing and fostering completely through until the second a representative leaves the business.

Definitely, with so much laying on the shoulders of one office, it's critical to your HR game should be totally first rate. In this preparation, we're demonstrating how to do precisely that. Around 30% of new workers surrendered in the initial three months of business. 13% of millennial workers would leave their place of employment on the off chance that they don't discover potential for profession improvement. 89% of HR experts concur that leading standard presentation the executives is more viable than yearly execution audits. These insights show that HR is an inexorably significant region that organizations should zero in on. Our course will comprise of a progression of basic conversation focuses. These are intended to cover this expansive theme as completely as conceivable to support development in these indispensable regions. What's more, to work with a genuine and productive conversation inside your association about how you can each develop this fundamental trademark .

Both at work and in your own lives by and large. A portion of these will be really protracted, and some will be somewhat direct and brief. At the finish of this guide comes the main last advance. Conversation time, don't skirt this. This is the main piece of this preparation. At the point when you finish this course you need to go through no less than an hour or so going over the inquiries we supply toward the end collectively. Whoever's the big cheese in the gathering should assign a facilitator whose duty it is that each question is covered and that everybody time allowing, can give their opinion, ensure all commitments are esteemed, all ideas considered, and all feelings regarded. So how about we move into the principal conversation point. Further develop your enrollment cycle. In case you're hoping to soar your business, you need to have the ideal individuals with you. They are a gathering of people who are sincere dedicated to your organization and will do all an option for them to make your business a versatile one. Additionally, you're completely certain that they will be with you eventually. To fabricate a group like this, you need to begin reinforcing your establishment while picking workers. To put it plainly, you need to put additional time in the enlistment cycle. recruiting workers is anything but a simple arbitrary determination of people, nor is it showing particular treatment to those supported. Maybe a powerful recruiting measure puts a sensible measure of time in pre work screening. This implies becoming acquainted with the possible worker however much you can study their experience. What do their previous managers say about them? Do they have a profession History is there anything in the data that may appear to be incorrect.

Additionally, focus on delicate abilities like proactivity correspondence and collaboration over aptitude and abilities. Keep in mind, a solid hard working attitude is more noteworthy than specialized abilities instruct representatives as the HR office, your primary objective is to keep up with the degree of joy and fulfillment of the workers. A compelling method to accomplish this is by offering them chances to foster their expert and individual abilities. This implies devoting a spending plan for instructive projects like online courses, meetings, and classes. Try not to feel that such exercises are only a careless method of going through the organization's cash. All things considered, treat it's anything but a motivating force and a speculation. In time your workers will master more abilities and develop more both as experts and people. This thus inspires them to continue to work for you. examine this with them to decide the best instruction you can accommodate every one so they can make the most out of it. set clear assumptions. Notwithstanding having an essential enrollment measure, there will consistently be a few representatives who are lazy unmotivated, and can even begin to be an awful impact on others. such people ought not go on without serious consequences as it will influence the group's confidence, which thusly can have significant strife in the organization's exhibition. To keep something like this from occurring, you need to set up clear assumptions from the beginning, set direct guidelines that are to be regarded by everybody. On the off chance that somebody's not ready to consent to the concurred norms, or is intentionally disturbing the work environment kinship, in all honesty, disclose to them the outcomes they may confront in the event that they proceed with their conduct and be firm about it. This will assist you with trying not to think again when you're compelled to fire somebody.

Work on motivation programs. Remunerating representatives for a job done the right way is a surefire approach to get them inspired. All things considered, as the HR director, their prosperity is your main need. Impetuses come in all shapes and sizes. Converse with your group and consider offering prizes for each achievement accomplished. You can take him out for lunch, surrender enrollments, rebate coupons, organization attire, and even help their own causes. However notwithstanding these, you can consistently remunerate them with the easiest yet most remarkable type of motivation. saying much obliged. Use HR is programming. HR organization can be a difficult, tedious cycle that includes a great deal of information and desk work. Luckily, there are a ton of devices accessible to improve on this cycle. To make the HR office considerably more productive. You need to have HR is programming. HR is or HR data framework is a computerized arrangement particularly appropriate for little to medium scale organizations that upgrade every day HR errands by overseeing and sorting out organization information. HR programming makes it workable for the HR divisions to save additional time and assets and distribute them to more productive endeavors. Is it accurate to say that you are hoping to incorporate hr rayas programming for the organization? Here are the top devices that you can look over Ukg Pro, attempt net, bamboo, HR, workday, human resources the board, Oracle, cloud, HCM and zenefits. Think about adaptable work choices. Preferably, representatives ought to be available consistently while working at their ordinary full time eight to five positions. Notwithstanding, this may not generally be the situation. A few organizations discovered that representatives will in general have lower confidence for not being allowed their own timetables. One of the HR division's duties is to keep up with usefulness among representatives. making acclimations to their plans for getting work done is an incredible method to do this.

All things considered, Exercising sensibility in the work environment is a method of telling the representatives that you care for them and that their government assistance is your first concern. How might you make such changes. You can do this by offering adaptable work alternatives. Here are a few choices that you can give to your workers. far off work, working distantly at home and utilizing video conferencing applications for correspondence. Substituting areas, alternating among home and office to work. Packed work week, representatives can abbreviate their work week by working more hours on different days so they can have additional downtime. changed work hours, representatives can adjust their work hours, however they need to finish the standard eight hour work day. low maintenance work, working 30 hours every week or less. Occupation offering dividing assignments and obligations to another worker while having a similar job. Flexi dinner time, representatives can pick an opportunity to eat and have a more limited break so they can leave early. Foster mindfulness for the organization's targets.

The essential HR office is subject to how well it connects to the organization's objectives. This is the reason have an intensive comprehension of your organization's destinations. This implies having a reasonable attention to your organization's central goal and vision, including its objectives and achievements. At the point when you have a total understanding into what your organization needs to accomplish, you can without much of a stretch eloquent it to your HR work force so they can adjust the division's destinations to the hierarchical objectives. give out successful criticism. getting criticism is intermittently disliked because of it having regrettable underlying meanings of deficiency finding and being harsh, yet, actually, giving out input and have an extraordinary effect on make individual and hierarchical progress. At the point when you give out criticism, it advances proficient development, further develops maintenance, and builds deals. There are two kinds of viable representative input, number one, building up criticism, the sort of criticism that urges a worker to continue to do a specific positive conduct.

At the point when we give this sort of analysis, we're verbally building up the beneficial outcomes of somebody's activities. Along these lines the deduction of the term model, something I truly respect about you is something I truly appreciate about you as I couldn't imagine anything better than to see you accomplish a greater amount of number two, diverting criticism, a sort of input that is as though we're advising somebody that we need them to quit doing this and begin doing this, suggesting the advantage of rolling out such an improvement. Model, do you have a second for some criticism? I'd prefer to give you some input is presently a happy time. As to, what do you believe is working out positively? or on the other hand What went poorly?

progressing worker input in the working environment is crucial in supplanting obsolete execution surveys, and moves the concentration in assisting individuals with creating developed criticism additionally fills in as an extraordinary instrument for you and your group in building an input cordial climate. Dispose of issue workers. Let's be honest, who doesn't have a solitary issue worker in the work environment? These many smooth laborers are the ones who are impervious to their work and their colleagues. Having miscreants like these can profoundly influence representative assurance, for they establish a poisonous work environment climate. Whenever left untreated, they can gradually tear others or much more terrible, destroy the organization. Unfortunately, a few organizations are too reluctant to even consider giving up these jerks.

The explanation is that some of them are really the top entertainers in the group. Hence, a few directors wind up undermining their qualities just to keep them. Try not to allow this to occur. On the off chance that you have questions about terminating such ones, an exploration paper from Harvard Business School will urge you to take out It says in contrasting the two expenses, regardless of whether a firm could supplant a normal laborer with one who acts in the top 1%, it would in any case be in an ideal situation by supplanting a poisonous specialist with a normal specialist by more than two to one. The point, discover who these and dispose of them quick, gather speed by proceeding to get these harmful individuals far from your organization. On the off chance that you do, you'll establish a quiet workplace. Execute work shadowing. Preparing is a fundamental part for HR directors. Nonetheless, when the word preparing is included, they frequently believe that it includes paying. However, that is not generally the situation. Workers can be prepared without spending a solitary penny. How could that be? work shadowing is a movement where a staff from one space of the association has the chance to work close by other staff in an alternate space of the association and gain knowledge from the experience. Workers participating in work shadowing will assist them with learning and develop inside their present job. At the point when you give work shadowing meetings to your representatives, they'll will see how different offices work. gain from the encounters of different associates.

Handle the significance of how different jobs support the association. Like different necessities and needs outside of their work job, acquire appreciation to various jobs and capacities inside the association. work shadowing assists representatives with mastering new abilities, characteristics and related capabilities that can be useful to their present job. Besides, being presented to various regions inside the association can help them acquire a more profound enthusiasm for how different offices work and how their jobs add to the achievement of the association. This thusly will assist them with developing all the more expertly. assist representatives with recognizing position explicit objectives. As the supervisor, you may have characterized assumptions for every representative, except it shouldn't generally be the situation. All things considered, toward the day's end, they know themselves better than you do. What you can do is request that your representatives distinguish objectives that are explicitly connected with their positions. At the point when supervisors perceive how their objectives orchestrate with an organization's targets, they should then rapidly assist them with creating activity intends to accomplish those objectives. Jobs differ in the work environment. Nonetheless, objectives much the same as usefulness and productivity are regularly viable. As you work with your representatives make it a highlight diminish blunders and lift usefulness. This thusly will save additional time, produce more deals and further develop your prosperity.

Apply the PTO strategy. Now and again, you may discover that specialists look bleak and discouraged. Furthermore, there could be various reasons why a few representatives feel that their work is only exactly the same thing again and again, as though being stuck in an unending circle. Then again, somebody may be managing disorder, loss of a friend or family member, relationship issues and other individual issue. Concerning others, they just can't just deal with the pressing factor of their work making them become worried and consumed. Assuming this is the case, then, at that point this certainly implies they need to take breather a vacation day from work can assist them with loosening up and reset. At the point when they get back to work. They will feel more revived and stimulated creating more attractive outcomes. As the HR chief, it's your obligation to ensure that workers reserve the privilege to take a break. You do this by took care of time strategy.

This strategy essentially implies that a representative has the privilege to have downtime from work while as yet getting paid. ptos incorporate occasions, days off, get-away, and individual matters, for example, loss leaves, jury obligation, and surprisingly military preparing. ptos give workers the opportunity to take vacation days as indicated by their carefulness. It likewise permits them to have some control of their timetable to take care of faculty matters. Sure enough workers will cast a ballot you the adaptability that they acquired through this approach. This understudy guarantees you that when they return, they will be more useful than never make a festival culture. organization culture is the foundation of worker maintenance, individuals will almost certain stay on the off chance that they appreciate each second of working there. Notwithstanding, low spirit might be a consequence of the absence of festivities in the working environment. For instance, perhaps your group arrived at another top in deals this month. However for everybody, it's anything but an update for them to work and work more. If so, then, at that point it's an ideal opportunity to roll out an improvement. At whatever point your group accomplished something for the business, feel free to celebrate, even in the little successes.

Attempt to have a good time office party after your group achieves an achievement or completes large ventures. The key is to set out more open doors to commend all the more regularly. For example, you can have an organization potluck and trade plans with representatives. social events like these expanded kinship and fellowship in the work environment. A few organizations likewise advance more modest, less authority occasions for representatives to appreciate. thoughts like open house, carry your canine to Work Day, National High multi day and public pizza day are incredible freedoms to have a work environment festivity. Another way you can offer basic thanks is by astounding workers with solid treats once in a while attempt to acquire sound and nutritious bites. Accomplishing something quite sudden for the workers is a method of saying thank you for a job done the right way. This will doubtlessly persuade them to continue to do their absolute best. approach them with deference. Regard is basic for a sound workplace. Treating workers with respect adds to their prosperity. At the point when you regard representatives, they become more ready, inventive and useful, along these lines bringing about a more certain working environment. So with regards to showing regard, consistently recollect, treat others the manner in which you need to be dealt with. So how might you make a particular work environment? Think about the accompanying show civility, consideration and amiability. Keep away from micromanaging rush to pass judgment. comprehend their restrictions. Pay attention to their sentiments. Monitoring your non-verbal communication, manner of speaking and disposition. Treat them reasonably and similarly. Practice compassion, regard others societies and convictions. Set KPIs as a HR director. One of your fundamental obligations is to guarantee that worker execution is consistently on an ideal level. You can do this by setting up KPIs. KPI or key execution marker is a measure that shows how adequately an organization is in accomplishing its essential targets. KPIs help to assess the accomplishment of arriving at their objectives. So how might you viably build up KPIs? This is what you ought to do. Compose a sound objective. Your KPI ought to be essential to the business. It should be lined up with what the organization is attempting to accomplish. Offer it with workers, correspondence is fundamental. Your representatives need to comprehend the objectives according to your viewpoint and how their assistance can add to the achievement of the organization. survey them intermittently. Check in your KPIs every now and then. This is crucial for keep tabs on your development and evaluate the organization's turn of events. You can do this on a week after week or month to month premise. Ensure it's significant.

Separation KPIs to make present moment and long haul objectives. altered to fit evolving needs. Associations adjust to new practices alter KPIs to supplement new changes. Update destinations. when required. Organizations develop and KPI ought to consistently verify whether KPIs are should have been changed or rejected right away. KPI measurements expanded Performance perceivability showing the individuals who are performing admirably and the individuals who are not. It likewise guides conduct urging a laborer to perform better. At the point when organizations use KPIs, it joins representatives to pursue shared objectives. It additionally helps in speedier dynamic. data gathered from KPIs can likewise help in creating future procedures for the business. What's more, presently it's conversation time. The main piece of this preparation whoever's the big enchilada in the gathering should assign a facilitator whose obligation it is that every one of the inquiries you see on your screen is covered and that everybody, time allowing, can express their opinion, ensure all commitments are esteemed. All ideas considered and all sentiments regarded.

Don't miss out!

Visit the website below and you can sign up to receive emails whenever B. Vincent publishes a new book. There's no charge and no obligation.

https://books2read.com/r/B-A-QWUO-WFHQB

BOOKS 2 READ

Connecting independent readers to independent writers.

Also by B. Vincent

Affiliate Marketing
Affiliate Marketing
Affiliate Marketing

Standalone
Affiliate Recruiting
Business Layoffs & Firings
Business and Entrepreneur Guide
Business Remote Workforce
Career Transition
Project Management
Precision Targeting
Professional Development
Strategic Planning
Content Marketing
Imminent List Building
Getting Past GateKeepers
Banner Ads
Bookkeeping

Bridge Pages
Business Acquisition
Business Bogging
Marketing Automation
Better Meetings
Conversion Optimization
Creative Solutions
Employee Recruitment
Startup Capital
Employee Mentoring
Servant Leadership
Human Resources
Team Building

About the Publisher

Accepting manuscripts in the most categories. We love to help people get their words available to the world.

Revival Waves of Glory focus is to provide more options to be published. We do traditional paperbacks, hardcovers, audio books and ebooks all over the world. A traditional royalty-based publisher that offers self-publishing options, Revival Waves provides a very author friendly and transparent publishing process, with President Bill Vincent involved in the full process of your book. Send us your manuscript and we will contact you as soon as possible.

Contact: Bill Vincent at rwgpublishing@yahoo.com www.rwgpublishing.com

www.ingramcontent.com/pod-product-compliance
Lightning Source LLC
Chambersburg PA
CBHW030537210326
41597CB00014B/1191